MW00464489

THE
SECRETS
OF
SKINNY

CJ KNAPP

The Secrets of Skinny, Copyright 2021 by CJ Knapp
Printed in the United State of America

Print ISBN: 978-1-7354674-1-2
Design by www.formatting4U.com

All rights reserved. This book is licensed for your personal
use only. No part of this work may be used, reproduced,
stored in an information retrieval system, or transmitted in
any form or by any means (electronic, mechanical,
photocopying, recording, or otherwise) without prior
written consent by the author. Any usage of the text, except
for brief quotations embodied in critical articles or reviews,
without the author's permission is a violation of copyright.
Author contact: CJKnappAuthor@gmail.com

For my beautiful sister – Barbara

Table of Contents

Chapter 1

Debby Tries Different Methods

Hello

My name's Carole.

I'm in my late seventies and slim.

I know you want to get rid of the extra weight you're carrying around. It's uncomfortable, unhealthy and unattractive.

Boy, do I have solutions for you.

And, I promise…no recipes.

The problems began in the 1980's. People were getting fatter.

The rise in obesity also saw an increase in type II diabetes. Perhaps you're already challenged with this disease, which affects every organ in the human body. The connection is undeniable.

Maybe you're holding at pre-diabetes, waiting for the other shoe to fall.

I have answers.

I've counseled people on weight loss, hypnotized people for weight loss and interviewed hundreds of people for weight loss. I was the representative for the United States and Canada for a company based in Ireland for bariatric surgery being performed in Belgium.

I can help you.

If you're reading this book right now, there is little doubt that you've tried many different diets. And, most of the time, if not all of the time, they've worked.

You've followed the diet rules and you've lost weight. For some of you, it may be the same five to twenty pounds of unwanted weight that you've kicked to the curb, over and over and over. For others of you, it could be you've lost a substantial amount of weight up to and over one hundred pounds.

Right? Right!

And, you know as well as I know what happens next. The weight you thought you lost, finds you again.

After enough time goes by, you will've gained back every last pound you worked so hard to shed and, horror of horrors, you keep on gaining.

Your next serious try at weight loss, sees you targeting a new heavier weight to strive for. You tell yourself: "I'll never really be thin. I want to be a healthy weight, one I can maintain, one I can live with."

Okay, now you're off to the races again.

You're planning to try a different diet; the latest. Maybe, you've gone back to your old familiar diet plan.

I know a woman who was in the same popular weight loss plan that gave her (accountability) as she had to check in and be weighed on a regular basis. She's since died; got to her goal weight, dozens of times. Lots of dozens.

After all, that old familiar plan worked before.

Yes, but did it? If you're back trying it again. It did not give you what you wanted.

Each time you try again, you lose again. And just

like clockwork, you gain again. In many cases, your weight keeps creeping higher and higher.

I've been privileged to work in the weight loss field for many years and interviewed hundreds of people, mostly women. People just like you. People serious about getting their weight down, becoming one of the slim ones.

Being overweight isn't just about how we look. It's about how we feel, how we function in the world and how we see ourselves. It's also how the world sees us. Right or wrong, it's a proven fact that in a situation where two similarly qualified candidates for the same job apply, the obese person will be overlooked in favor of the thin one. Similarly, at a singles dance, with a lot of women to choose from….Okay, I don't have to finish this scenario.

Let me tell you, I've been a program manager for a popular dating service and interviewed many many men asking them what their preferences were for a mate; first word out of their mouth was "thin."

I have a lot I want to share with you, but first I want you to meet Debby..

She's going to demonstrate this part of S.O.S.

If you're a man reading this, call Debby "John," making slight changes in the obvious places.

First let's explore some different diets with Debbie's help. I won't spend too much time on any of them, because you could've easily written this part of S.O.S yourself, but I want to make a point.

Fat free diet.

Debby's cutting all or Most of the fats from her diet. She's buying fat-free pastries and baked snack foods. She eats only lean fat-trimmed beef and skinless chicken broiled. Debby's losing weight!

After sufficient time has passed with Debby obsessed with eliminating the Devil fat from her diet, she's also close to her target weight. A few months pass and she's pulling clothes from the skinny side of her closet. But, wait a minute, she still does not want to bring those (fat) clothes to the Goodwill. Because, she thinks "what if?" "That was an expensive pants suit, good at hiding my belly. I'll just push the fat clothes further back in the closet.

Can anyone see what message Debby is sending to herself?

Okay, now it's seven months later and Debby's wearing the pricey pants suit, when the bug to diet hits again.

"I'm not gonna just cut out fats. Besides, we need some fat in our diet. The good fats are good for your brain. I'll avoid the bad fats, the saturated fats."

"I'll go on a no-carb diet."

And so she does.

No more carby snacks, no more potatoes, white rice or bread. She finds herself eating hamburgers without the bun, bacon, eggs, steak and whipped cream. And wow, miracle of miracles; she's losing weight. Again!

However, she watches her neighbor eating a jelly doughnut with her coffee and has all she can do not to grab it from the woman's hand and punch it whole into her mouth.

She starts to crave simple carbs. She also notices a lack of energy along with an unrelentless obsession to deify doughnuts, breads and potatoes. She dreams of birthday cake, piled high with butter frosting and wakes up in a sweat. Debby loses weight.

Half a year of this passes and then it becomes clear. This is not working as the house of cards falls in and Debby gains weight again. First a couple of pounds, then five, then ten.

She thinks "What's so bad about being a little plump? I'm fine the way I am."

Maybe she is!

But, Debbie goes to Bermuda with her husband and is shocked by how uncomfortable she is in the coach class airline seat. The safety belt cuts into her stomach.

After arrival at their vacation destination, she pretends not to notice the difference between how the women on the beach look and how she looks in the hotel full length mirror.

Debby redoubles her resolve.

She tells herself; "I will lose this weight. I will not live my life as a fat person."

She sees an ad in her local newspaper:

LOSE WEIGHT WITH HYPNOSIS

One Session and start eating less

Lose that extra weight like MAGIC

Debby's ecstatic. "Hypnosis…why didn't I think of this before?"

She keeps that night free of any other commitments, and drives downtown to the hotel where the event is scheduled.

The conference room is immense. There are rows of folding chairs set up and she sits in the front, thinking it might be better if she's closer to the hypnotist. She's a little nervous, not knowing exactly what hypnosis might do to her. Her husband told her he "loves her just the way she is and not to come home, quacking like a duck." A very common misconception about hypnosis.

She soothes herself thinking the advertisement said it was hypnosis for weight loss.

She's desperate now. She'll try anything.

Once comfortably seated, she looks around at some of the other attendees and see many women of all ages and all degrees of being overweight from slightly chubby to those that would be classified as morbidly obese. She secretly credits herself with not being "that" fat. The audience is about ninety percent female.

After a short introduction by a tall skinny woman, the hypnotist comes out on stage. He looks like a normal, slightly balding, middle-aged man. He starts by dispelling the common myths about hypnosis. He mentions old classic movies that show hypnotized subjects committing acts of crime or even violence against their will. People begin to relax as he makes it clear that no one can be hypnotized against their will and the hypnotist can never make a person do something that person would not normally agree to do.

There's an almost imperceptible dimming of the lights and the hypnotist begins to relax everyone in the packed auditorium.

Debby feels less nervous, quite calm and knows she has slumped a little in her gray folding chair. She's asked to picture a beautiful place in her mind and she's able to do this easily. She's surprised to note that she can still clearly hear the hypnotist's voice and is very aware of her actions. The thought occurs to her that perhaps she's really not hypnotized.

When the hypnotist asks her to see herself

thinner, she becomes distrustful. Why this is nothing more than "visualization."

This doesn't work.

She thinks "I've tried this before and I know it doesn't work. Debby's mental "guardian" has taken over and is cynically critiquing every sentence, every phrase, every suggestion. She is now "preserving" her "everyday Debby" ego. Her usual self.

Her overweight self.

The possibility exists that this critic will let some of the new hypnotized thoughts in and if this happens, she may leave the meeting and truly not feel like stopping for a fast-food burger and fries. Well, not that same night.

The beliefs we hold have, in a very real way, been hypnotized into us as one all-powerful, all-encompassing belief.

That belief is: It's hard to get what we want, whether it's money, a mate or a skinny body.

I'll get back to this later.

I am a nationally certified hypnotherapist and speak to you with years of experience.

Hypnosis only works if you give your full cooperation. A hypnotist cannot do it for you or to you.

Now, Debby tries diet pills.

She figures if these are sold over the counter or prescribed by her doctor, they've been okayed by the FDA and are safe. She thinks it's worth the risk. She's desperate. She's willing. She tells herself her health will benefit from being thin and that outweighs any negatives or side effects. "Just till I get my weight down, then I'll stop the pills."

Debby is once again ecstatic. "wow, this is easy. I'm never hungry. I can just drink coffee and a small amount of food every day."

However, Debby doesn't feel well. She has a case of diarrhea which seems to be getting worse and she feels dizzy and headachy. Looking in the mirror produces a slight gasp. Dark circles have appeared under her eyes and her skin seems to have changed, losing it's tone, becoming almost saggy, making her look ten years older.

She's losing weight, but feels terrible. She's often irritable and snaps at her husband and children.

She goes online and looks up the weight loss pills she's taking and is alarmed at the number of side effects. Dropping weight rapidly includes losing muscle mass. Your heart is a muscle!

Not able to continue, she gives up on this method and once again, Debby is depressed over her inability to lose the weight that continues to plague her and is increasing each year.

White knuckle weight loss:

With a brand new resolve, Debby joins a gym. She's intimidated by all the size fours and size sixes floating around the gym, but she's determined.

Exercise!

The new weapon in her arsenal to fight the fat she hates. She's glad to find the ladies locker room has private stalls to change in. She can't help but sneak peeks at the trimmed and toned bodies of some of the other women. "Where is their belly?"

The first week, she gets to the gym four times and finds it altogether pleasant, even enjoyable. The women are friendly and helpful. This lasts for three weeks.

Then life interferes. Her son needs a ride on her gym days. She has to work extra hours on a new work project and gas prices have risen. It takes longer to prepare healthy dinners and she has an ingrown toe nail, the parking lot is always too full, not to mention her key fob won't work at the gym's entrance.

The excuses mount. The next payment is due on her membership and what the heck, she hates getting sweaty and having to wash and blow dry her hair. The city water is hard, doesn't make good suds. She can just as easily take walks at home and buy some weights to life in her basement.

So three months after Debby's resolve, the great workout volley ends.

More common excuses:

Oh, I think my metabolism died.

Everyone in my family is heavy. It's in the genes.

It's probably my thyroid.

I hardly eat anything and keep gaining weight.

I eat healthy, so don't understand why I'm fat.

I used to exercise and was thin, then I got sick, had an accident, my husband left me, my husband died, I retired, went on vacation, 9-11 happened, too many holiday parties, daytime's Okay, but night-time comes and I want to reward myself, I'm a stress eater, I'm a nurse and eat out of emotions because of all the pain I see, I'm a third shift worker, I'm a waitress and eat the restaurant food, I eat out a lot, I eat home a lot, I travel a lot.

And so Debby is stymied.

Maybe you are too.

Keep reading.

Chapter 2

QUESTIONNAIRE

1. WHEN DID YOU FIRST DECIDE YOU NEEDED TO LOSE WEIGHT?

2. WHAT WERE THE RESULTS OF THAT FIRST VENTURE INTO DIETING? A BRIEF ANSWER WILL SUFFICE.

3. HOW SOON AFTER YOUR FIRST TRY DID YOU LAUNCH ANOTHER DIETING ATTEMPT? A GENERAL ANSWER WILL BE FINE.

4. HOW OLD ARE YOU?

5. ARE YOU MORE THAN 10–25–50–100 POUNDS OVERWEIGHT?

6. HOW LONG HAVE YOU BEEN TRYING TO LOSE WEIGHT?

7. DO YOU HAVE A FAVORITE DIET? DOES THAT DIET WORK LONGER FOR YOU? WHY DO YOU THINK YOU FAVOR THIS DIET?

8. WOULD YOU BE MORE AGREEABLE TO CHANGING EATING PATTERNS IF YOU COULD KEEP IN ONE OR TWO OF YOUR FAVORITE COMFORT FOODS OR "FUN" FOODS?

9. WHAT MAKES YOU "BEGIN AGAIN" TO LOSE THOSE UNWANTED POUNDS. YOU MAY HAVE SEVERAL REASONS.

10. HAVE YOU NOTICED A PATTERN? IF SO, WHAT IS YOUR PATTERN? PLEASE TAKE THE TIME TO EXPLORE THIS ASPECT OF YOUR DIETING LIFE.

Chapter 3

Types of Diets

Atkins: This diet is predicated on the "fact" that carbohydrates are used for fast energy and any carbohydrates that aren't used in a short period of time will be stored as fat on our bodies. It also consists of upping protein and cutting down on all carbohydrates. Carbohydrates turn into sugar after they're digested. Needless to say, sugars must be eliminated as much as possible. There are different levels with this diet. The most difficult is called "The Caveman Diet," and allows only high protein foods, non-sugar drinks and very little else.

Scarsdale: This diet was popular in the 1970s and is not too dissimilar to the Atkins Diet. It incorporates stereotypically healthy foods, such as fruits and vegetables and low-fat dairy products. A typical dinner would be a piece of meat, some cottage cheese and a salad.

Weight Watchers: This well-known diet came into being in the 1980s and has many Weight Watchers quarters throughout the United States. It has enjoyed a popularity that has waned somewhat in recent years. The concept is that each food is assigned a point and a certain number of foods are allowed each day that add up to a pre-determined number of points; the objective to lose weight. If you go to the Weight Watchers center, there is a weigh in and there will be a motivational talk by a weight counselor. Participants are encouraged to reach their "target" weight.

Jenny Craig: Jenny Craig is another method that appeals to people who prefer to have their food choices taken away from them and know that they are eating what they are "supposed" to be eating. With this diet, you buy food from Jenny Craig and don't have to do a lot of thinking or planning as it is all done for you.

Limited Foods Diet: Grapefruit diet, Cabbage soup diet, Mango diet, Brown rice diet, and anything else you can think of that limits the variety of foods that you are allowed to eat. When you can only have mangos, you will soon get pretty sick of mangos and not feel like eating. Your appetite becomes jaded when facing one more bowl of cabbage soup.

Zone Diet: This is one-third protein, two-thirds carbohydrates and a little fat.

Mediterranean Die: These meals are built around plant-based foods with a small amount of meat.

Makers Diet: This is based on biblical principles. Don't eat soy. Buy their products.

Rosedale Diet: This is similar to the Atkins diet; another low carbohydrate diet. You're encouraged to force your body into ketosis by cutting out most carbohydrates and ingesting healthy fats for energy needs. It recommends fifty to seventy-five grams of protein per day. Also, many supplements are highly recommended. Coincidentally, these can be purchased from Rosedale.

Diet pills: These can be doctor prescribed or over the counter appetite suppressants. Short term results that often have the person feeling jittery and may even be detrimental for the heart.

Blood Type Diet: In 2013, a major review concluded that no evidence exists to support benefits of the Blood Type Diet. End of story on that one.

Sensa: This is a product that works solely on our "sense of smell" to lose weight. It purportedly does this without the person changing their normal eating and/or exercising habits. Dr. Alan Hirsch MD, founder and neurological director of the "Smell and Taste Treatment and Research Foundation" states; "Contrary to what most people think, hunger is not controlled by your stomach, it's controlled by your brain, specifically the hypo-thalamus." He also says "certain scents can help set a motion into a process that triggers your hypothalamus to send signals telling your body, you've had enough to eat. Dr. Hirsch developed 'Tastant Crystals" that could be sprinkled on your food to enhance olfactory input." He says, "that will imperceptibly speed up the natural satiety process, which prevents overeating." What? You never heard of this one? There's more.

Fasting: It takes twelve hours after your last "feed" to enter into a fasting state. The easiest way using this method, is to count your hours that you spent sleeping at night. This means no breakfast. Get it? Break-fast. And right here, let's explore the myth of breakfast, being the most important meal of the day. It isn't.

Lipo-Suction: Sometimes we want to reduce certain areas of our body, usually for women, centered around hips, thighs and in some cases, as is similar for men, the abdominal fat. This area can have an outer layer of soft adipose fat and/or a layer inside consisting of more adipose fat surrounding our internal organs. This is the white or bad fat. Adults have some of the "good" fat and it exists around the shoulders and neck. You can increase this fat, which is also in your muscles, by exposure to cold temperatures. The lipo-suction method utilizes a process consisting of vacuuming out the superfluous white adipose fat. Problems with this are, we will put the fat back on. In addition, we may be grotesquely mis-shaped after this. The interference with the natural shape of our body and fat may be put back on in a less even fashion. We could end up being very disappointed with the whole lipo-suction experience. I've personally seen proof of this. While interviewing frustrated overweight people, they've pulled their shirt up and revealed lumps and cave-ins on their flesh. Many of them cried.

Nuphedrin: This product contains real South African Hoodia in twenty times the normal strength used. Patented as Advantra-Z-r and SlimaLuma-3. This is another pill or supplement method.

Flex Belt: This is a rather pricey abdominal-toning flex belt device. It works by delivering electric muscle stimulation and is cleared by FDA, believe it or not.

Pritikin: Based on good food choices, with some foods labeled "Caution" foods.

Packages Delivered foods: Nutrisystem delivers food to you. Don't try to take your packaged foods into your favorite restaurant or even to your in-laws.

Gastric Balloon: A balloon is inserted through the esophagus, then inflated. It remains for six months.

Gastric By-pass Options: This is extreme. People do this to end the torturous battle with obesity. There are several different procedures you can opt for to use surgical means to lose large amounts of weight. They are dependent on our present state of health and how much weight we need to lose. Lap band causes a restriction that is in your body for life and could malfunction. Vertical gastroplasty is a one cut general anesthesia surgery. The short-limit gastric by-pass is a slower weight loss than that the other by-pass surgeries. A gastric by-pass can be performed where your stomach is made smaller, your intestines may be cut in half, with the bottom attached to the stomach. This sometimes causes a "Dumping" syndrome. There is a Sleeve Gastrectomy for the morbidly obese. Sixty to eighty percent of the stomach is removed. This is sometimes done before a full gastric by-pass. These are major surgeries.

And on and on and on.

Why are there so many diets, yet still so many overweight people? You can answer that question. What do you think?

Keep reading for my answers.

17

Chapter 4

Understanding Exercise

Some people love to exercise.

To these people, this word means jogging, running, numerous trips to the local gym where you "work out." Maybe you take a class with others, because that motivates you; could be aerobics, maybe even the once more popular Zumba class. Or the class where you ride a stationary bike, commonly called a spinning class. Perhaps you swim laps in a king-sized pool. A real gym-rat. Yoga anyone? Palates?

If you eschew the gym, you might rise early, put on your athletic shoes; used to be called sneakers, and do your running or bicycling right out of your front door.

Now, not everyone "loves" to exercise.

However, "everyone" thinks it's good for them and tells whoever will listen, they're planning to start exercising; get back in shape, though they've never actually been "in shape."

Okay, so let's look at this from a new perspective.

According to "The National Center for Health," less than twenty-five percent of Americans over the age of eighteen get enough exercise.

So, will you ever find yourself in a Zumba class?

Commonly in such a class, there is a very perky 19-year-old instructor bouncing around and choreographing new moves every forty-five seconds to a pounding, ear shattering, infectious Latin beat. Yes, you will? Okay, have fun. No? Really didn't think so. I did one once. I liked the music.

How about running five miles every morning, before your coffee? Or, lifting barbells every other day? Swimming? You would? Okay, better you than me. Nope? Why? Water gets up my nose and the waters too cold. Hmmmn.

All right, enough of that.

We live in a physical world.

We have a body.

Our body is, or should be, precious to us as it is how we maneuver in this physical world.

Do we have to do planned organized exercise?

If you are inclined, that's just fine. If not, keep reading.

Actually, keep reading anyway.

We are living in physical bodies in a physical world.

Bodies move. That's what they do.

Dead bodies no longer move. That's a fact.

But, live bodies like ours move.

You do have to move your body on a regular basis. Not just to go from your computer screen to your car.

I, as a writer am often guilty of too much time on the computer. My thriller novel "Who Took Hannah" is waiting patiently for the sequel, which be published after S.O.S.

It all comes down to doing what you're willing to do. Think about that sentence please.

We must use the body we have. We can

accomplish a lot of improvement without changing a lot of things.

We can happily live our lives with small changes.

For instance, stretch before you get your day going. Do it before you even get out of bed. It will feel immediately good and you'll wonder why you didn't do it sooner.

When you're upright, touch your toes, or however close you can get to your toes.

Open your arms and push your elbows back and take some nice deep breaths.

Now drop your arms and look left, right, up and down.

Do a few squats (look it up if you're not sure what that is).

Now, we've moved everything. Maybe five or ten minutes have passed and we feel better for it. This is the perfect time to say your mantra. It doesn't have to be out loud. You can think it to yourself. Just as good.

We have to think, not in terms of "exercise" but in terms of "movement."

Easy to use the stairs, walk more, help the clerk bag the groceries. We're just moving.

We have to move our bodies more.

Think of a car just sitting and getting rusty.

It doesn't have to be the Daytona 500; it just needs to be started and driven around the block on a regular basis.

It makes no sense to have great elaborate exercise aspirations if we don't do them; if we won't do them. The same philosophy holds true as does with diets. We don't need to over-do, just to do it and be relaxed about it.

The body-consciousness is aware of and finely tuned to itself, which is ourself. It's on the job and will let you know if you're pushing too hard. Go to any gym or race track and count all the ace bandages. These folks didn't listen to their body. The body-consciousness is what leaves our body on physical death. It's no longer needed after we die. It continues doing its job while we sleep.

I won't elucidate. That's a story for another book.

It's exceedingly beneficial to re-evaluate our understanding of how to treat our body; how they were devised to be treated. They are to be used, not abused.

Just use your body. Move your body.

Keep it authentic. Keep it real.

Chapter 5

Addressing our Beliefs

We talk to ourselves all the time. And we talk to others. We're always cementing messages into our awareness. The things we think and say are communications of what our beliefs are and absolutely impact our world, our life and yes, our bodies, our weight.

Here are some examples. See if any sound familiar.

- I've always been fat.
- I have a low metabolism.
- My whole family is overweight.
- It's my thyroid.
- It's baby fat. Ever since I had my kids, I can't get rid of the baby fat.
- I'm in menopause.
- I'm in peri-menopause. It's middle-age spread.
- I hate salads.
- I just love food.
- I eat one doughnut and gain weight.
- I'll start eating healthy after (fill in whatever applies)—you name it.
- I'm never hungry.

- I hardly eat and still gain weight.
- I gain more every time I get on the scale.
- I got my mother's genes.
- I got my father's genes.
- I just have bad genes.
- I look awful.

This is a very incomplete list. Add your own.

Here are other very different phrases to think and say to yourself.

- I'm happy, healthy and whole.
- I keep getting slimmer.
- My health is important to me.
- It's easy to lose weight.
- I eat well and don't gain weight.
- My pants are loose, need to go down a size.
- I can eat dessert when I want to.
- I'm thin and beautiful.
- I love my body.
- I have a fast metabolism.
- Just being alive keeps me thin.
- I have good genes.
- I look great.

Which list of things do you think will serve you better?

Does it make sense to say the things on the second list, even if you don't feel like you believe them? Even if you feel like a hypocrite? Even if you feel silly?

Yes! Yes! And Yes! Fake it till you make it!

Decades of studying how we create our own reality, including the body we live in, leaves us with this conclusion.

- We create from the inside out.
- We also cannot ignore the next sentence,
- We also create from the outside in.

Thousands of books have been written espousing both methods.

Creating from the outside in has taken precedence for most of us most of the time. What to eat. When to eat. How much to eat. Recipes and more recipes. What combinations to eat. Never eat this. Always eat that. Portion control and on and on and on. You know the gig.

Then along came the books that begged to differ. The Gurus. The New Age movement, The CDs that challenged everything you ever believed. The instructors who taught us how to visualize and imagine the bodies we wanted, not to mention, whatever else we want. Act as though you already have it, or him, or her and soon you will. You were advised to leave a cup of coffee and a piece of pie out, waiting for this mysterious time traveler to show up at your breakfast nook. This perfect being you've manufactured in your mind.

Many have attempted to apply these instructions, only to fail and then be down on themselves, believing they weren't evolved enough to create what they desired.

Okay, this is where the rubber meets the road.

I will meld both of these concepts so you finally not only lose weight, but prosper in other endeavors.

I've given time and ink to creating from your inner Subjective self to your physical or Objective self.

It's a process.

I intend to give you all my physical or Objective secrets also.

Both are in play.

Do I believe we always create from the inside out? That is, from the Subjective to the Objective.

Yes!

Is it possible to always succeed?

Yes!

Is it probable to always succeed?

No!

Until you can hold out your empty hand and announce to yourself and the Universe the word "apple" and VOILA it appears on your palm, then we as a human species are not "There" yet. You need to understand outside to inside and inside to outside. Remember, inside is Subjective and outside is Objective.

Now, back to the apple: do we do this magic act in the inner (subjective) worlds?

Yes!

You can use the dream state as an example. Think it. It's there. Imagine it. It appears. Want to be elsewhere? You're there. Travel at the speed of light, no faster. Crave looking twenty years old? Yep, no problem.

Go back in time. Go forward in time. You are not dealing with time and space as you acknowledge in this world's constructions. You can even experience "simultaneous" time. Oh yes, commonly known as deja-vu. You can experience this in the physical or objective world. This is a little trip on the time track, where any time period can be in the present moment.

So, what are we mere mortals in physical bodies supposed to do?

Okay, first acknowledge to the best of your present ability, that we create our own reality and our own body.

This is Subjective to Objective.

Stop trying the old and the new diets.

This is Objective to Subjective.

Keep this book handy to refer to. You'll slide away from remembering what I'm teaching here.

Here are some things to keep in mind. Human beings love methods. Don't forget this is a world of process, not like the inner worlds, where things can appear with only a thought or desire. This is a world of time and space. We process our reality. That is the proof we live in a physical world where time and space are aspects of our existence in this world.

We manifested here to experience this world. We wanted to come here. Yes, it was our own idea. Isn't that just so amazing?

It's all good.

First, we are creators.

Do not doubt this.

Can you create that darn apple immediately in your empty hand?

No?

Okay, then keep reading.

Chapter 6

Why Listen to me?

I've spent my life studying how reality is created.

At the age of seven, I mailed away for a pamphlet promising answers to life's big questions. My mother threw the booklet away, saying the Rosicrucians were devil worshippers. She believed my interest was a result of being in the Catholic orphanage she'd placed me and my two older brothers in. I had just been released to live with her and a new stepfather. Actually, I wanted answers that weren't forthcoming from the nuns and priests. I knew there was more to know.

My goal is to pass on my knowledge and experiences.

I wondered, as an adult, how someone could weight 600 pounds and not eat more than I ate. I applied for and took a position as Admissions Director for a nursing home. I spoke with desperate people who weighed a quarter of a ton or more, often with two blown knees, barely able to walk and also barely eating. They were dieting lifers. A morbidly obese woman I admitted to the nursing home was drinking eight to ten gallons of water a day. Yes, gallons. The nurses were hiding water from her.

I also took a position at a weight loss company and interviewed hundreds of potential clients. Most of them told me they were "never hungry" and had tried "every diet going."

They were still fat.

An interesting fact: the three foods most people named as most disliked were Brussels sprouts, fish and liver. The three most loved: chocolate, pizza and ice cream.

I want you to benefit from my lifetime obsession on how we create our own reality.

This book you hold in your hands can be a source for making your life more enjoyable. You deserve it.

I've chosen to focus on the issue of weight loss because the problem of being overweight is so prevalent in the USA and spreading to other countries.

Why?

It's because of our inability to generate our own happiness, to be content in our own skins.

Chapter 7

Consciousness and Life Attitude

Consciousness creates form!

Wow!

What a mouthful.

Will you believe it when you see it?

Or

Will you see it when you believe it?

The typical approach for changing something is to change or amend something physical in hopes that other physical changes will occur.

This is the thinking behind all dieting.

Example: If I stop all sugar, all breads, and night-time snacking, I'll lose weight.

Okay, not bad. Sound instructions. Have you tried that? Are you thin?

The more we understand how reality is created, the more we're able to swerve from the universal information banks or mass beliefs and expand to new understandings.

We can accomplish our desires using the concept of mind creation coming before physical manifestation.

Okay, that was a loaded sentence.

Important to understand there are all kinds of

"stops" on this particular subway to complete and total "creation at will" or "conscious creation."

Try to find where you fit in on the continuum. There are wide variations between trying every diet on the planet, including starving ourselves, to the other end of the spectrum, looking in the mirror at our overweight body and telling the reflection; "Skinny now." Pause. "I believe."

Many people have been hurt on the rocky shores of "you create your own reality" and blame themselves for failing. If you're not happy with all you have manifested, and are still creating plus size jeans and four X pullovers. Take heart. The buck stops here.

Here I want to tell you a story I've heard from several different sources that might clear up what I'm saying, if you're scratching your head.

A man was traveling in the great Northern African Desert, seeking truth and spiritual enlightenment. He had need of a place to stay for the night. He came upon a small oasis where there was available a tent for sleeping quarters to rent. Water, a nice meal and a comfortable cot would be provided.

The man had previously heard stories of camel stealing marauders who roamed the desert at night. The man's camel was very important to him for his journey and mission.

Now it happened there was a holy man who was also the proprietor of the desert inn.

The traveling man wasn't sure what to do in this situation. He fervently wanted to place all his trust in his higher power or universal God source as he chose to call this concept. Some simply name this "All that is."

He asked the avatar what he should do about his prized possession; his camel.

The holy man sat cross legged and arranged his cream-colored robes comfortably around his knees and leaned forward from the low fluffy cushion and said with a twinkle in his deep brown eyes, "Trust in God And tie up your Camel."

So, I want to teach you how to do both at the same time and not have it constitute a conflict for you.

Thoughts/emotions/feelings

All this needs to be said again and again and again in different ways!

Your mind is a prison full of doors, barred to all outside with "you" the only inmate.

Consider these.

It is or is it possible for me to become, a singer, a writer, a fine artist, the heavy-weight champ, the president of the United States?

Let those ideas sink in.

"I can't" and the doors are locked.

"I can" and the doors swing free.

Okay, I can hear you now.

I'm a 60-year-old woman. I could never be a boxer, let alone the heavy weight champ. Okay, you are likely right. Some things are beyond the realm of a probably reality. President of the United States? Who knows? Maybe.

When we contemplate these objectives, there's a current of fear. Fear is debilitating. Some of us are more sensitive to this emotion of fear. It has a proper place and works like an instinct for survival if we sense danger. Or and this is important, fear perceived where no danger exists, steals our energy and motivation.

33

To strengthen your mind and thoughts, be aware of what you put into them.

Monitor what you watch on television, what you read in books, newspapers, magazines and where you frequent, and all of that includes monitoring time spent with friends or relatives. You know who those people are. If you're not sure, be aware of how you feel after having spent time with them, in person or on the phone. You won't deceive yourself. You'll know.

Remember when the year 2000 was approaching? Predictions of gloom and doom were everywhere. None of it ever came about. It didn't happen. Were you affected by those attitudes?

Conversely, stay open to strengths. Be with positive people, watch positive television, and movies. And again, avoid negative relatives, within reason of course.

Move your thought current to the infinite. That's where creation takes place. Send good thoughts out and watch them come back.

You cannot ever create yesterday.

You cannot ever create tomorrow.

You can only create Now.

The point of power is in the present. Give thought to this. Right now; create tomorrow. You can't! Right now: create yesterday. You can't! You can remember and you can plan, but you cannot create. You can create right now!

It will happen for you quicker and quicker.

It's not necessary for exhausting mental machinations. It's more of a relaxing and allowing.

Courage and presence of mine are the same thing.

Cultivate a knowingness in the moment and a command of the mind and all will come to you.

A lack of mental control is cowardice. Success is based on courage. Failure is based on doubt.

Cultivate courage, always adding to your repertoire of strength.

Become deliberate in all things, speech, walking, writing, eating, all things.

Become cool and relaxed, not hurried and fearful.

Don't panic with set-backs. If an interruption of your plan occurs, give it relaxed energy and it loses its force or control.

Chapter 8

Some Practical Steps to Think About

I'm not going to neglect approaching weight loss without getting up close and personal with the practical things to do on a physical level.

Here are both aspects of the same concept. These are the steps toward weight loss success.

- One: Step–mental–Cut back on all Negative input
- One: Step–Physical–Cut back on sugar
- Two: Step–mental–Increase positive input, music – humorous movies
- Two: Step–Physical–Cut back on white flour
- Three: Step–mental–Read something positive/ uplifting am and pm
- Three: Step–Physical–Explore different vegetables
- Four: Step–mental–visualize yourself thinner
- Four: Step–Physical–Include fruits, fresh or frozen or sugar-free in cans

More on sugar

Research has verified that sugar is addictive.

Professor of psychology John Hoebel, at Princeton University did an experiment using rats. They were fed a diet consisting of 25% sugar and experienced extreme withdrawal symptoms when the sugar was taken away, including extreme anxiety with shaking and chattering teeth, similar to human beings going through withdrawal from nicotine or morphine.

It appears, according to Dr. Hoebel, that foods high in sugar and fat trigger the brain to release natural substances called "opiates", that stimulate "dopamine", a pleasure chemical our body naturally produces.

A craving is set up. Once sugar has been eaten, more will be craved.

Repeat, once sugar has been eaten, more will be craved. Like attracts like.

Neuroscientist Ann Kelley also has done some sugar research using rats. Rats are used because their brain chemistry is similar to humans. Not attractive, I know.

Ann Kelly's rats were fed sweet meals and then later they were offered two bowls of food. One sweet, the other contained healthy food. The rats always chose the bowl of sweet food, showing again the predilection for repeating sweet eating behavior,

High sugar foods cause your sugar level or glucose level to rise in your blood rapidly. To process this, your pancreas produces a hormone called insulin to clear the sugar out of your bloodstream and send it to your body cells. Some goes to your muscles for quick energy, some to the liver where it is stored in the form of glycogen for future energy and the rest gets stored right in your fat cells.

How much clearer can this be?

When you stimulate your pancreas this way, it produces too much insulin and this causes your blood sugar to plummet. So now, you have all this extra insulin swimming around in your blood stream, looking for more sugar to work on and this causes a craving for... you know what I'm going to say... Yep, more sugar.

You are programming yourself to eat more sugar by yep, eating sugar.

All that extra insulin your body just produced will now store fat for you.

Let's also be aware that this extra insulin will damage artery walls, making it easier for fat and the bad cholesterol to stick, to build up inside your arteries and precipitate heart disease.

Sugar has no redeeming qualities. It causes you to feel fat, bloated, tired and depressed and does nothing good for your teeth.

Is it worth it?

Large doses of sugar raise the production of galanin, a protein made by the brain that influences appetite and eating by increasing your bodies preference for both fats and sugary carbohydrates.

Your liver will produce enough glucose for kidneys, brain, muscles and nervous system when it processes healthier fats and healthy carbohydrates. There is no need for refined sugar foods.

So, the next question is about artificial sweeteners. Which one? How much? Safe or unsafe?

- Sucralose, Equal, Splenda
- Aspartame
- Saccharine
- Erythritol, sugar alcohol
- Xylitol, sugar alcohol
- Sorbitol, sugar alcohol
- Polydextrose, sugar alcohol
- Mannitol, sugar alcohol

If too much of any of these are ingested, often diarrhea will result.

Stevia comes from the leaves of the Stevia plant and is the most wholesome of sugar options. It's natural, not chemical. It grows in Paraguay and other tropical areas of the Americas. Its leaves are super-sweet and remain stable even after having been dried. Stevia leaves have been used to sweeten beverages throughout South America for centuries. Interestingly, you may purchase seeds to plant from Amazon. I just ordered them, so cannot report any results yet.

Put succinctly, of all these possible sugar substitutes, only Stevia is proven to have very few side effects.

All should be avoided,

Stevia may be used within reason.

Chapter 9

Some Basics

Proteins: Every one of your cells need protein. The basic structure of protein is a chain of amino acids. Protein repairs your body's cells and makes new ones.

Fats: Dietary fats are essential; support cell growth, protect organs, keep you warm. Fats help your body absorb nutrients and produce important hormones.

Carbohydrates: They provide energy, store energy and spare protein and fats for other important uses.

Ten of the best healthy proteins:
1. Black beans
2. Eggs
3. Cottage cheese
4. Turkey breast
5. Quinoa
6. Fish
7. Pistachio nuts
8. Greek yoghurt
9. Almonds
10. Lentils

Ten of the best fats:
1. Avocados
2. Cheese
3. Dark chocolate
4. Whole eggs
5. Nuts
6. Extra virgin olive oil
7. Chia seeds
8. Fatty fish
9. Full fat Greek yoghurt
10. Coconut oil

Ten of the best carbohydrates:
- Lentils
- Oatmeal
- Beans
- Berries
- Quinoa
- Nuts
- Brown rice
- Vegetables
- Barley
- Chick peas

In your grocery store you'll find many other foods to enjoy.

If you love bread, I recommend Ezekiel bread, made from sprouted whole grains and legumes. It's tasty and the healthiest bread you can eat.

Pasta lovers can opt for whole wheat, or my own personal favorite; Barilla Red Lentil Penne. If your grocery store doesn't carry it, request it, or go to Amazon.

If you love your soda, here's what I drink every day. Zevia is my constant sipping partner. Fourteen flavors; my favorites are Cola and Black Cherry. I like the Ginger Ale also. Amazon has this too.

Almost ten percent of the United States population has diabetes.

Sugary beverages are the leading cause of added sugars.

I also use liquid Stevia in my coffee. Stevia does not raise blood sugar levels as noted in the Journal of Clinical Endocrinology & Metabolism.

Breakfast

After interviewing hundreds of people and discovering what they eat in the course of a day, it was no surprise, most said "I'm not hungry in the morning, but I know breakfast is supposed to be the most important meal of the day."

Poppycock!

Something important to note is, the proponents of "Intermittent Fasting" for weight loss, advise you to continue the fast when you wake up, instead of breaking the fast. If this appeals to you, it's a method that has merit. Barring any personal health problems that don't permit this, of course. Fat burning begins approximately twelve hours after eating food and escalates between sixteen and twenty-four hours. There is much written on this for you to explore. Don't go overboard.

Success is getting and staying slim.

Much depends on changing your beliefs.

Your weight also responds to what you do.

Please understand, both are valued paths.

Religion has long recommended praying to God for what you want.

Weakening this method by saying "It has to be a faith sized request for it to come to fruition." There are various other qualifiers also. Some would say it has to not be selfish.

For my purpose, I want to make the point that even religion recognizes the truth that reality can be manipulated depending on our beliefs.

I'm not predicating it on a God figure.

Here's a typical day of what I eat.

- **Breakfast**: Coffee with milk and Stevia. Ezekiel toast and lots of crunchy peanut butter.
- **Lunch**: A whole can of tuna fish with onions, celery and mayonnaise and Zeevia soda.

Or

A whole can of garbanzo beans with added tomatos and veggies

Or

Two hard boiled eggs in a huge romaine lettuce salad with olive oil and vinegar

- **Dinner**: A large bowl of red lentil pasta with olive oil and grated parmesan cheese. Zeevia
- **Snack in evening**: Veggies with melted cheddar cheese, and a piece of dark chocolate—LINDT 90% cocoa, a piece of fruit and if I'm hungry, a bowl of oatmeal.

I personally don't eat meat, for philosophical reasons. I never eat so much that my stomach hurts. And, I recommend Metamucil daily if you suffer from constipation.

Generally speaking, I'm against unnecessary pills. I take a multi-vitamin, a B complex and Ashwagandha daily.

You want to know if I've ever been fat. Right? People often ask this of me.

I've seen my weight go up and been unhappy with that. It feels very uncomfortable. You feel it when you walk, when you move, when you try to roll over in bed.

The diet I tried was Atkins. It was a disaster. I was eating bacon, whipped cream and hamburgers. (This was before I stopped eating meat.) I felt weak and wanted a doughnut or at least an apple for crying out loud. My weight went down, then plateaued. "You all know that one." I was aware all the time that I was dieting. I constantly urinated on the little Keto stick to see if I was in Ketosis. In other words, I became obsessed. As soon as I ate anything "Off" the diet or normal, my weight shot up. This was a long time ago and I still should have known better. I had temporarily forgotten that dieting does not work, because it presupposes that you are fat. So, here I was gaining more pounds than when I started.

When I finally came to my senses and stopped the insanity and remembered that I was a thin person. I knew the dieting was making me crazy and making me gain weight. I was truly amazed at how true it was, that dieting makes you fat. I became 100 percent convinced of that.

I want you to start thinking of yourself as a thin person.

Chapter 10

Beliefs

Can a diet work if we don't believe it will work?

It can "achieve" short term results, but because the energy isn't there to continue, and the reasons, "excuses" for it not to work will proliferate; it will eventually fail. It won't give you the slimmer body you crave. You have a right to be thin, if that's what you desire.

We're all familiar with the placebo effect. Statistics overwhelmingly prove over and over that when a group of participants are given a substance or a pill to achieve a certain outcome, and in a double-blind study, some people in the group are given an actual pharmaceutical product, the results are amazingly similar.

Why do such a large percentage of people given a "sugar" pill achieve the hoped for benefit?

In a word... expectations.

The point here is to make the case that what we are conditioned to expect will materialize. The weight we believe will return will come back with a vengeance.

We've tried so many diets that work short-term.

We must understand how our beliefs and attitudes create our world.

Please understand, this is not about the power of positive thinking. More about that later.

We aren't targets of misfortune. We are active creators of our lives.

When we observe something; it changes. The observer affects the observed. Seeing affects the seen.

Reality changes the moment it's observed. It reflects our assumptions, mirrors our beliefs.

The observer and the observed create what we call the objective reality.

Some people may know this without knowing they know it.

Recall my Rosicrucianism pamphlet. I wrote for this over seventy years ago. I've been searching for truth from a very young age.

My objective with S.O.S is to pass on the knowledge and personal experiences I've acquired through years of seeking and share what I know, so others needn't spend so much time and energy squeezing information about life and our existence and our innate ability to direct our individual needs and desires.

My mission is to provide a source to make our lives more enjoyable.

I've chosen to focus on the issue of weight loss because it's so prevalent in the USA and becoming more so in other countries, partly because of our inability to generate our own happiness and joy; unfortunately, too many of us get mired in the dieting cycle.

I'm aware there are books on the shelves and online that will tell you that it's your thoughts, the way that you think, that will make you gain weight. These pundits will say they've stayed slim and swear that you can do it too, if you will only listen to them and trust them.

Is this true?

Absolutely!

Can you do it?

Absolutely!

Will you?

You tell me.

Have you tried and failed? The bottom line to this story is that it's absolutely possible, but not necessarily probable. I will come at the problem from both sides of the equation.

So, to reiterate, can you get skinny and stay skinny if you think skinny thoughts, while dining on cheeseburgers, fries, chocolate cake and ice cream?

Okay, let me put this another way. Can you watch a video on levitation by an East Indian Savant who levitates at will and then go out on your lawn and begin to rise steadily while in the lotus position?

Or, can you read an account about Uri Geller, who can bend spoons into a perfect U-shape with his bare hands and then grab a spoon from your cutlery drawer and bend it in half?

Are these things possible for you to accomplish?

Absolutely!

Will you be starting a new career in the entertainment circuit levitating or bending spoons?

Probably not!

Can you read a book about getting thin using self-hypnosis, and a certain woman named Esther Ordinary, who went from a hefty 240 pounds down to a svelte 115 pounds and has remained that weight for many years. You say, "Wow, why can't I do this?"

You can! Will you? Hmmmmm, be honest here. Pause. I rest my case.

You know thin people who seem to eat whatever they want and yet they stay thin.

What's different about these people?

Are they constantly monitoring their thoughts? Are they chanting under their breath, I am thin, I am thin, over and over. No, that's not it.

So, what is it?

I could say they "know" they are thin and will always be thin. However, that will immediately lead you to ask the question; "how do I get to "know" I'm thin."

Here we start to get down to the nitty gritty, the bare bones, the meat of the matter; the actual story of creating what we want. That's a body that can wear jeans, tuck our shirt in. A body that can mount stairs without laboring, get out of a car quickly, fit easily into restaurant booths and airline seats and sexy shoes.

Okay, if it isn't our thoughts, then what is it?

Is it our beliefs? Our beliefs about ourselves, our bodies, the food we eat or don't eat, the world, the universe as we perceive it?

Where did we acquire these limiting beliefs that don't serve us well, don't work for us? Beliefs that don't provide us with the benefits we so earnestly crave. Beliefs that undermine and sabotage our desires for a slim healthy body,

So, where do we get these beliefs?

Everyone, everywhere, everything!

Some beliefs were handed down to us in early childhood. "Looks like Ginny inherited the fat gene. She'll be heavy the rest of her life." Some others are…

If you eat after seven pm, it all turns to fat... or... Too bad she was breast fed, now all she wants to do is eat constantly... or... people like us of... you fill this in... descent are always fat.

Some beliefs are held en masse by most people. "As soon as you hit menopause, it's all over, middle-age spread and never see your feet again." "After childbirth, you keep most of the weight you gained and each subsequent baby leaves you still fatter. Baby fat...you mutter"...or I just have a slow metabolism. Or It's my thyroid, or the older I get, the fatter I get, and on and on and on.

Will this work the same for everyone? Of course not! We're all different. We have different sets of beliefs. It would appear at this point in our discussion that the next order of the day is to simply change our beliefs.

Sounds easy, doesn't it? So simple. Just change your beliefs and change your reality. Once again, possible but here is the kicker, not probable. Why? Because we create our world from our beliefs and they cannot simply be done away with. Our beliefs form our perceptions and most of this has been handed down to us either by family, friends or the world.

So, where do we start?

First, by realizing that our beliefs are not wrong. Our beliefs are not bad. They just are.

We cannot function in this world without our beliefs. It is the nature of this physical world. It is how we create our world, our life, our reality.

To start, we must begin to recognize or uncover our beliefs. Many beliefs are connected. If we have a belief that we must be attractive to be loved and being pencil thin is the main criteria for being attractive, then ipso facto, we need to be thin to be loved. The belief that grows from this belief is that at our current weight we not lovable, not loved. What a conundrum. And we wonder why we're depressed.

In order to begin to instigate change, we have to recognize and lay claim to our beliefs. We have to accept that they exist. Accept the reality of them. This may be a process and we may have to do it over and over, but it is absolutely doable.

Once we feel we have accomplished accepting our beliefs, we begin to take away their power. We neutralize them. We embrace them as ours and a part of who we are. Many that were hidden from us are now visible. We see them. We can begin to fix what we'd like to change.

Consciousness is life. It shows in our attitude.

Consciousness creates form!

Wow, what a mouthful or should I say "what a mindful."

You will have heard some version of the things I am about to tell you. Some of the things I say will be familiar to you. Some of you will have simply dismissed them with a slight roll of the eyes or a "Yeah, right" look on your face.

Some of you may have a conscious understanding that there is likely some truth to the things I say here, but are not able to put it into action. You think only people who have special gifts can make those things work. Maybe people who've been meditating and chanting all their lives can make their reality change into what they want it to be. There is a wonderful saying I repeat here.

Whether you believe you can or believe you can't; you're right.

Chapter 11

More about Beliefs

Remember, beliefs aren't necessarily bad. Not at all.

Beliefs are how we create our life, our world, our reality.

Everything does not have an intrinsic meaning. We ascribe meanings to things, based on our beliefs.

Again, beliefs aren't bad.

My beliefs might be different from others, but our truths are the same.

Reality is a truth. Light and color are truths. They exist on all dimensions and for everyone. Though we may interpret them differently. Most fascinating of all, love is a truth. However, this truth, in this physical world, is only a pale imitation of the place it holds in importance on all dimensions. There are numerous beliefs distorting this truth here on planet Earth. This is definitely a story for another book.

Does Allah exist on all dimensions? Does Christ? Does Santa Claus? Does getting fat if you eat late at night exist on all dimensions? These are beliefs.

You cannot hope to change your world by totally dismissing and discarding beliefs. You can learn what they are and that will help define who you are. Plato, a student of Socrates employs the maxim "Know Thyself." Great advice indeed.

When you uncover your beliefs, they will have less power over you. You may still hold many of the same beliefs.

A word about hypnosis here. This is a way to find out more about your inner workings. But, be remembering that your inner and outer—subjective and objective—work together. They work in tandem. They are not enemies.

During a hypnosis session, there is a shutting down of the outer reality and life as you know it on a daily basis and a reaching into the inner self that is not affected by the ego and habits and beliefs.

Changes can be made at this level, however once the ego re-claims control, the danger of reverting back to previous behaviors can take over again. This is often the case.

There may be powerful beliefs making a person overeat or drink alcoholically or shop compulsively.

You may use the information in this book to apply to those and other issues also.

After reading this book, I hope you've made inroads to the place where you live.

I hope you've identified some limiting beliefs and avoided getting down on yourself for holding those beliefs. Again, you cannot live this life without holding beliefs. You will never be completely without beliefs in this world.

Don't substitute hating yourself for a belief for which you don't approve. Just accept it. It was probably handed to you. Or perhaps, you devised it to help with a problem in your life that may no longer exist.

Example: To avoid an overly demonstrative, or worse, stepfather; you began hiding in your bedroom and became reclusive. Maybe you piled on the pounds to be less attractive.

Perhaps you were told to be quiet when you had something important you wanted to say and you're still weighing your words to see if they're acceptable enough to be spoken out loud.

Maybe your mother said, within earshot, "She's so darn clumsy." Now, you never dance, not even alone in the kitchen, though those words may have been forgotten on a conscious level.

Or your father said "He'll never amount to anything, he's just worthless." What a horrible message. Then comes a self-fulfilling prophecy for Junior.

Too many art teachers have squelched creativity in their students and snuffed out a future Picasso or Georgia O'keeffe.

You get the drift.

Chapter 12

Practical Notes and Stories

I'm keeping my promise that this is not a RECIPE book.

Neither is it a fact-bloated tome.

You won't get a certificate in science or medicine.

It is a combination of physical and meta-physical. By meta-physical, I don't mean new-age. There are no angels, crystals, seances, good fairies or channelers.

We burn most of our calories just living. This means breathing, maintaining body temperature, heart pumping, all organs functioning, including the brain.

There is a misconception that exercise is equal to food ingested for weight loss.

Picture the Indian guru, sitting alone on the sidewalk begging for a few coins or scraps. He's skin and bone and rarely moves at all.

Now picture some of the pudgy exercise instructors you've seen at your gym, when you've been going there. They could be teaching three or four classes a day and are still chunky.

Some studies link high insulin levels to weight gain. Elevated cortisol appears to contribute to high insulin levels and glucose, producing an army of prediabetics. Current thought relates increased cortisol levels to stress; real or imagined.

Isn't this what we're talking about with examining our beliefs about life? What are you stressing about? Can you fix it right now? This minute? If so, do it. If not, let go of it. Just let it go!

Remember if you believe you'll always be fat, then, you'll always be fat.

Is it another person you're worrying over; a cheating partner, an alcoholic teenager, a dying parent? You cannot fix another person. Ever! You must allow them their journey. I know first-hand how difficult this is.

You cannot act in the past. You cannot act in the future.

The only place you can act is in the present moment. It is not possible to do otherwise. The point of your power is right now. The point of power is the present.

In this world "Like attracts like" the old-fashioned way of saying this is "Practice makes perfect."

The first time is a leap of faith. You knit a sweater, you bake a pie, you have a baby, you run a marathon, take a job, give a talk at a seminar.

Now you have the consciousness to do those things. This will make it easier and more productive to continue doing those things.

You've dieted, lost pounds and gained them back. You now have the consciousness to continue doing exactly that. Diet…lose….gain. Diet….lose….gain.

You have to step off that merry go round.

Realize you can have a brand-new consciousness.

You can't keep moving in the same circle. Everyone now knows the definition of so-called insanity is to do the same thing over and over and expect different results.

You must break away. Break the pattern.

I know you can.

Remember—Like Attracts Like. Make that your mantra.

You always create more of whatever you're paying attention to.

Therefore, if you are paying attention to having to diet because you're fat, you will create more of having to diet because you're fat.

But, if you're paying attention to, and again, this is "Not" the power of positive thinking, this is authentically moving in a new direction, so if you're paying attention to what you're accomplishing, what you're enjoying, what you're satisfied and happy with, you will create more of that.

Remember the movie about the middleweight boxing champion Jake LaMotta? The title was "Raging Bull." Robert De Niro had to gain a great deal of weight in a short period of time for his role. He admittedly ate pasta and pizza and got very fat. When the role was completed (An excellent movie by the way), he, in very little time lost the weight he wanted to lose. He knew he could. He had gained sixty pounds. His first "intent" was to get fat. Then his "intent" was to get rid of the fat. It wasn't a problem.

He was slim.

He got fat

He got slim.

He didn't blow up again.

How much does the past affect the present and the future?

How much are you allowing the past to affect you now?

You have power in the present. That's the point where reality is created.

Don't bring up the past in your present.

Don't worry about the future in your present.

Your point of power is the present.

Chapter 13

For the Sake of Clarity

Here's a typical day of what I eat. Exactly.

- **Morning**–Coffee with half and half and Stevia one slice of Ezekiel bread toasted loaded with crunchy peanut butter and thin layer of sugar-free jam
- **Mid-morning**–two colas sweetened with Stevia
- **Lunch**–A whole can of tuna fish made with mayonnaise and red onion and lettuce on Ezekiel toast–two slices, hot tea with half and half and Stevia
- **Dinner**–a whole can of Garbanzo beans cooked with tomatoes and greens and topped with Parmesan grated cheese and Stevia Cola
- **Evening**–A glass of red wine sometimes, peanuts or other nuts and Stevia cherry soda or 2 packages of instant oatmeal with Stevia and Cashew milk
- **Later**–this varies–clementine or apple and slice of cheese–sometimes potato chips, sometimes dark chocolate—I prefer Lindt—90% cocoa.
- **Brush teeth** – go to bed

I weigh myself on a regular basis. I know there are proponents of not weighing yourself, except perhaps once a week. I understand that thinking, but I don't agree. I know that whatever I eat on Tuesday will be on Wednesday's scale.

Whatever I eat on Sunday will be on Monday's scale.

I know myself very well and know there may be some sneaky beliefs that have hung on having to do with eating whole coffee cakes and gaining weight.

I take none of it too seriously.

I laugh at myself, amused at my folly if I see the scale go up. It's not serious. It's not permanent. I don't fret. I don't beat myself up. I simply don't eat another entire coffee cake. My new belief is that I'll gain weight if I do that.

It's a conscious decision if I do decide to eat another sour cream Jewish coffee cake……which you may have guessed is a true story; knowing I'll find it funny and stop that again. This goes for spooning in an entire half-gallon of cherry vanilla ice cream also. Then, I'll stop doing that.

It's not a diet.

It's a frame of mind.

We have choices.

Let's return to clarity on the practical side.

This is the physical side.

Remember though, it is "always" inside to outside, subjective to objective. We are, or at least, I'm not, able yet to hold out my hand and say "apple" and watch one appear.

So, generally speaking, you can happily have two starches a day. A starch or a carb is one potato or one slice of bread or one normal serving of pasta. You needn't be obsessed with this. It's a general note, not a rule. Ezekiel bread can be two slices easily. And, no, I don't have stock in the company.

You can have four proteins a day, more if you're a larger person. A protein is one pork chop or chicken breast or small ice cube size of cheese or a can of tuna or a small can of beans or a serving of other fish.

You can have two fats a day. A pat of butter is a fat. Don't stop fats. There are many great fats. Check your list. Your brain needs fats. You need them.

And, you should have all the veggies you want.

I have a glass of red wine two to four evenings a week. You can have a dessert and count that as your starch if you desire. Probably not a half-gallon of ice cream.

Do not get obsessive with any of this. It's just a general idea of what a person would eat during a day. Don't starve yourself. Make yourself eat. You need to eat. You should never be walking around hungry. It is not necessary. You do not want your body to start hanging on to every calorie because it believes there is a famine.

Don't bother with breakfast if it doesn't appeal to you.

Have your food whenever you want to eat it.

It does not matter if that is later at night.

Do not obsess.

When you go on vacation; eat, drink and be merry. Eating habits are likely altered, but not so much that you can't eat out in restaurants. You're on vacation!

One note: all creamy things are a waste. They all are about one hundred calories per tablespoon and usually don't taste that good anyway. I've eliminated them entirely for decades. That includes bottled salad dressings. Yech! I have oil and vinegar or oil and lemon. I like the salty taste and have used no-sodium salt for years.

I prefer a nice grilled salmon with a clean baked potato and veggies not swimming in a greasy camouflage. Add a salad and it's perfect and you won't get hungry afterwards, or feel sick from creamy greasy who knows what. I do have a glass of wine most of the time, but dessert only very rarely, which after you kick the sugar addiction, you won't even crave sweets.

Remember like attracts like. The more you eat sweets, the more your body and taste buds will clamor for them.

In the same vein, the more you eat clean foods that look like themselves, a piece of fish, a potato, a carrot, a pile of steamed broccoli, the more you will only want those things.

Like attracts like.

The more you do it, the more you will do more.

Chapter 14

In Conclusion

Is reality created from the outside in or from the inside out?

Do we create our own reality?

Can we right now always consciously create our own reality?

Key word is "Consciously." Qualifier is "Right now"

Can we get better at creating our reality with full awareness?

Yes!

Do we still create our reality with little or no awareness?

Yes!

Herein lies the conundrum.

Step back for a moment. Visit your past.

Recall maladies that plagued you earlier in your life. Did you suffer from frequent colds? Did you have constant sinus infections? How about migraines? Diarrhea, cold sores, specific allergies? What about debilitating shyness?

Have some of these or any of your own personal afflictions, disappeared?

Just went away. Like magic! Like a miracle! Maybe you haven't thought about those maladies in years. Think about them now.

Well, you healed them yourself.

We all do healings constantly.

I have done some with full consciousness. Those are stories for a different book.

You chose S.O.S. to help you lose weight. You want to get off the dieting merry-go-round.

You are creating your own life. You're not a victim of circumstances.

It's fine to look back at your history, but don't get stuck there. Look, but don't stare.

Continuing to hold on to old hurts and grievances is like dragging a dead body along with us everywhere we go. It's a heavy load and like a cadaver, it begins to stink. Others can smell it also. Stop resurrecting it. Don't give it energy. It stinks. It serves no purpose.

Your pre-conceived notions have a perception formed by your beliefs.

Give some thought to how many times you say "I'm sorry." "Pardon me." "Excuse me."

Stop yourself and notice when these exclamations are uttered but are not legitimate. Of course, sometimes they are appropriate.

Begin noticing what you're creating. Look around yourself; where you live, what kind of vehicle you drive, or ride in. Look at your body, your hands, your feet. Look at the people in your inner circle. Your world on the outside (objective) is a reflection of your world on the inside (subjective.)

Now, let the full understanding that you are creating all of it begin to permeate your entire being.

With awareness, you'll become more efficient at consciously choosing what you are creating.

When you make these truths your own, your whole life can change.

Once you know, you cannot go back to not knowing.

A powerful confidence begins to become your constant state of being.

Others will notice. Be prepared for that.

"Something's different about you. I don't know what it is, but I wish you'd give me some of it."

Others will be attracted to your more aware self.

This book is marketed as a diet book, but if you're still with me this far, you know it's so much more.

You each have a reason for reading it. What else do you want to change in your life?

What are the things you've been telling yourself you'd do, once you were thin?

Start!

You can!

Don't listen to people who are shouting negative beliefs. Even if they're family members.

Some people might be jealous of your success and try to tear you down, rain on your parade. Don't let them. Block them from your consciousness.

Protect your mind and filter what you let in.

Soon, you'll be appreciating the benefits of your new life.

Go shopping. Buy new clothes, new shoes and maybe some bright red lipstick. Have lunch with a friend. Life is to be explored and enjoyed.

We're here to have experiences, not to suffer.

Suffering is only good if you learn something from it and then leave it behind. It's not a necessary factor for growth, though it does often precede growth. Hence the saying "No pain, no gain." Do not take this literally. Find a mantra that resonates with you. I'll share mine later.

Don't be discouraged by slip backs. Remember there are many mass beliefs that compete for your attention.

Read this book again.

Soon all of this will be who you are. The new you. The you who accomplishes. The one who gets what they want in life.

Here are some sayings or mantras that will serve you well.

Let a smile be your umbrella.

Just direct your feet to the sunny side of the street.

Life is just a bowl of cherries.

Singing in the rain.

Just what makes that little old ant think he'll move that rubber tree plant?

He has high hopes. High apple pie in the sky hopes.

Here's mine: I am happy, healthy and whole, good energy flows through me unencumbered.

People often say to me "You never gain weight, but never diet, what's your secret?" They also ask if I'll be their mentor.

Now I can answer "Please read my book. Read S.O.S."

"I wish you all success!"

Dear Readers,

This little book is meant to combine the physical and the non-physical worlds. Understanding how this works will help you create a life that you like.

Please visit my fineartamerica.com website for more on this subject. - carole-johnson.pixels.com

Author website: CJKnappAuthorBooks.com.

Please email me at CJKnappAuthor@gmail.com with comments or questions.

All the best,

Carole Knapp Johnson

Books by CJ Knapp

<u>Fiction</u>
Who Took Hannah?

<u>Non-Fiction</u>
The Secrets of Skinny

Made in the USA
Monee, IL
17 April 2021

64849305R00049